T0365770

And God Answered....

Rod Guerrero

Balboa Press books may be ordered through booksellers or by contacting:

Balboa Press
A Division of Hay House
1663 Liberty Drive
Bloomington, IN 47403
www.balboapress.com
1-(877) 407-4847

Because of the dynamic nature of the Internet, any web addresses or links contained in this book may have changed since publication and may no longer be valid. The views expressed in this work are solely those of the author and do not necessarily reflect the views of the publisher, and the publisher hereby disclaims any responsibility for them.

Any people depicted in stock imagery provided by Thinkstock are models, and such images are being used for illustrative purposes only. Certain stock imagery © Thinkstock.

ISBN: 978-1-4525-8470-6 (sc)
ISBN: 978-1-4525-8471-3 (e)

Library of Congress Control Number: 2013920529

Printed in the United States of America.

Balboa Press rev. date: 11/15/2013

BALBOA.
PRESS
A DIVISION OF HAY HOUSE

God Answered....

     I have written this book to help you understand the richness of all that resides within you. I have discovered that I have always been rich and I desire for you to discover your own richness. The richness I speak of is the richness of LOVE. Refer to this book when negativity is creeping into your thoughts, which create your words and actions. The best time to refer to this book is before that negativity reaches into you and takes over your thoughts, which will lead to words that inflict pain or worse yet, cause you to do actions that inflict pain upon yourself or others. Dear loved one make no mistake inflicting pain upon another is to inflict pain unto yourself, read through this book and open it up to any page before your mind gets carried away with your negative thoughts.

     I may not have met you but I know we are the same when pain enters our lives. We allow ourselves to get defeated in sadness, depression, despair, loneliness and ultimately self destruction. These are terrible places to be and there is a way out of those places through love. Negativity is not you and life need not be a struggle for you. I desire your life to be filled with love, peace and prosperity and to know that you have always been loved more than you can ever imagine.

     The love that is within you is so great it can never be fully contained, for it is the love within our entire universe and that is always expanding just as you are. You are an inexhaustible supply of love and you will be guided to unleash that authentic power within you that will set you free. Let's give love to one another and make our travels through this life a beautiful one, you see dear loved one, I will tell you a great secret and it is that I am you and I want you to know from the depths of my heart that I love you. If you want to see a miracle, something so beautiful, so incredible, so inspiring, you need to look no further than the nearest mirror.

     There are poems throughout the book designed to be cut out and hung up to inspire and remind you to awaken, I am honored that you have chosen to read this book, thank you for your time and attention.

Since I was a child I felt there was something not right with this world as if we were existing contrary to how our existence was meant to be, I always felt this seperation, a sadness in my heart for the condition of our world and how we treated eachother. We have wars, poverty, famine, disease, racism, genocide and much negativity that surrounds how we view life. Along with this there was the fear that is constantly perpetuated in our media as well as how at the root of all religions around the world is to love each other and yet we have been slaughtering each other for thousands of years by the millions in the name of God.

I held a belief that we were alone and separate and that somehow God had forgotten about us. I had a broken heart for humanity and a burden I carried that I was helpless. In that helplessness I became depressed and bitter toward myself and my world and thus began my spiral into addictions of all sorts to escape the pain I felt for years. This lead me down a horrible path of addictions and self abuse with alcohol, drugs, food, sex, material things, mindless entertainment, thoughts of suicide and whatever else I could use to fill the enormouse void I was feeling, yet nothing of this world could fill that emptiness I felt.

Eventually running from the pain and heading toward a path of self destruction I ended up divorced, going to rehabs, getting DUI's, arrested and being filled with so much fear and feeling so much pain, yet throughout all these life experiences I was always calling God…. I never received an answer. It wasn't that God wasn't answering, it was that I never had the patience to sit and listen to God. So I began to sit quietly and listen, and I asked God why have you abondoned me, where are you?

And God Answered: My dearest loved one, I am here, I am always here, we have never been apart, for we are one. To be separate is just an illusion you have accepted in your mind and you have chosen to exist this way and in that belief you created your seperated self or what you term the ego. The ego is that unsatisfied voice telling you this illusion you created is real and you are alone and must fight to survive and that to survive fear, hate, anger, greed, resentment and even killing are justifialbe for your survival and that oneness, love, forgiveness will make you weak and vulnerable, the ego tells you to attack in order to survive.

I tell you now my child nothing can be further from the truth, for love is your essence and that love is a light within you that can restore you to wholeness and bring forth heaven upon earth for you, if you let it. Your life was meant to be one of joy and peace created from the love that is you. Only love is real in this reality that you perceive, everything else is an illusion that you have projected and it seems to be real, although it is not. The only real presence that can truly be real is the love you give into this reality and it is through love that you were created and it is from my love that is your essence that gave you existence.

My source of love is the only true existence and it is from this source that you asked to go and experience all that is and your illusion of separation began when you allowed fear to enter your joyous experience. This illusion of separation that you believe in is what brought your reality into existence. This illusion is perpetuated by your belief in separation from everything and that feeling that you are alone. Your ego or separated self holds onto these falsehoods to keep the illusion of separation going and keeping you from awakening to your true reality, that which is total love. My child you are never alone and there is no separation, there is only oneness and complete connectedness through love. You my child can choose to live in love right now at this very moment. No matter what your circumstance may be, choose at this moment, as you hear this to mentally, emotionally and physically reside in love. Quiet your mind at this moment and hold thoughts of love toward yourself, simply think to yourself, "I am love."

Me: Who or what am I?

And God Answered: You are because I Am. Know now that you and I are one. I Am all that is, for I Am the existence of all, for there is no-thing that is created from any other source, form or substance other than that which is I. I Am the eternal I Am, which includes all beings, which includes you, I Am you. I Am the energy that gives life and form to all matter. I am that which is beyond energy, the all that is from where energy sprang forth. Everything in the universe is an extension of my energy that is vibrating at varying degrees of speed, this includes you as well. I Am the I am when you state who you are or what you desire to be. I Am the universal mind which holds all thoughts and creations and I endowed you with my likeness to create anything your thoughts can imagine through your mind. I am you, we are one, and the potential that is within you is beyond your capability to comprehend. It is our desire together for you to now awaken at this time to your true and full potential, to awaken to the God being that is you, that is, us as one.

I would like for you to think a thought, now exactly where did that thought come from? Have you ever stopped to "think" where your thoughts are coming from? What is the source of your thoughts? Know that I Am original thought, I Am first cause of all that is from that original thought, know that my original thought and only thought was every possible thought that can be thought and this was first cause to all creations throughout all realities, universes, dimensions of space and time and beyond. Know that you are an extension of that first thought, the first and only I Am. Know that you and I conspired to conceive that which is you, this concept in my original thought which gave conception to you, your birth, your existence. This was a perfect concept of creation, which is simply for you to know me, through me and I to know myself, through you.

This may be difficult for you to understand but to awaken to this truth there must be a purification of your thoughts and for you to hold complete love for the self. We are united through self love, there can be no other way, for this way contains all ways for us to awaken together to our truth, which is I Am the I Am that awaits for you to awaken to the truth you hold within you, which is….. "I Am God".

Me: Matter and energy are one and the same and beyond that is the I Am from where all stems from. All that exists can be traced down to a vibrational energy that moved it into form and that vibrational frequency pervades the entirety of all that is created in this Universe and so unifying everything as one, which makes me one with God?

And God Answered: Yes.

Me: So that would make us all one with God?

And God Answered: Yes.

Me: That would make me and every other being one with everything that is creation and all one with God?

And God Answered: Yes, yes and yes.

Me: How can I hold thoughts of love for myself if I can't forgive myself for all the horrible things I have done? All the lies I have told, for all the blame I have put upon others, all the judgments I held against others, the guilt I have made others feel, all the pain I have caused to others. I can't even look at my reflection in the mirror, let alone love myself, I think that I am not worth Gods love and I deserve to be punished.

And God Answered: All your fears and pain simply stem from lack of self love and you my child just answered your own question. You "THINK" you are not worthy of my love and that's where your fall from grace began, in your thoughts. My dear child every single obstacle in your life that causes you pain all began at the level of mind, for your mind is the builder of your world. When you accept fully within your mind that only love is real, you will know it is the only true existence that there truly is, and your most powerful creative point.

It is from love that the Universe was created and held together perfectly just as you are, it is from love that you were created. Love is your essence and it is an investment that must be tended to within you from your thoughts, through loving words and loving actions toward the self. Love is the most powerful creative force that is, for it is the only force that is. Love is a powerful attractor for love, love attracts love, love is what's only truly abundant within you. Pause throughout your day and quiet your mind from busyness and reach inward to bring forth that love, it must be given and it will be returned many folds.

Love is the answer to all your fears, for all your problems can be quickly and peacefully resolved through love. Love will free you from the veil of fear that has blinded you into fearful reality that is being created by you. Love is the portal to the truth of who you really are, your home, your true existence. Love is what you are.

Y-O-U-N-I-V-E-R-S-E

You are perfect and complete, you are much more than you realize, you are forever. For you there is no beginning and no ending, you have been here since the beginning and everything that is resides in you. You are the entire existence of all. In truth there is no beginning or ending there is only NOW, this moment and you are always recreating yourself at each moment of now. There is nothing but ONE and nothing else. The energy that makes the sun shine is in you, the force that moves our oceans resides in you and the love that lets flowers grow graceful is you. Know you are part of something so inspiring, something so far more than your five senses, there are no words to describe it. You are more beautiful than you can possibly imagine, so perfect, so complete and so powerful, you hold the beauty and the magnificence of the universe within you; in fact you are the UNIVERSE!

I Am Awakening

Me: So lack of self love has created so much of my negative problems, my unhappiness, and my pain?

And God Answered: Yes.

Me: So how can I begin to undo all the unhappiness I have created?

And God Answered: Your mind is the portal from which thoughts are born. When thoughts are repeated within your mind, those thoughts move outward through your emotional expressions. This literally begins to arrange people, places, events and circumstances into reality, you are doing this at every moment whether you are conscious of it or not. The simple thought that you state of being unhappy is what is creating you to be unhappy, why not make a conscious effort to choose a better thought toward yourself and hold it repeatedly and have that as your state of being. Would you agree that a sad thought makes you sad and a happy thought makes you happy? And when you think a funny thought it actually moves your body to smile and laugh? For laughter could not happen without being born within you as a thought. Every emotion you feel or action you take is precipitated by a thought. For all decisions in your life are simply strings of thoughts pulled together which you came to a conclusion upon to take action and thus creating what you experience.

A thought you should repeatedly think is "I Am Love" and I would encourage you to hold that thought repeatedly in your mind throughout your waking moments. For you see you are the full creator of all your experiences through the thoughts you are thinking over and over repetitiously in your mind. When you connect your emotions with those thoughts, your thoughts become empowered, energized and literally begin to move matter into form. Your thoughts create all your experiences and everything is being projected from within you. You are the only creator of your reality and no one else can do this for you other than you. Know the power that is your thoughts, for your thoughts are creative and are always creating at every level of your existence.

Simplicity is important for you to know, for nothing in nature struggles or resists, nature is being nature. Ask yourself what your current state of being is now? To do this is to be consciously awake and aware of yourself. There is simplicity in being and that is to simply think and feel that which you desire to be. Whatever you are thinking and feeling at any moment is simply your state of being and if held long enough, you become more of that. Consciously choose your thoughts and energize them through your imagination. Visualize the being you desire to be and through your emotions feel as if you already are who you desire to be. Think it, feel it and become it, this is your creative potential.

Me: What is it that I am supposed to learn or what test do I need to overcome to be free? I am frustrated and upset, I am worried and just see more of the same every day, more and more struggle. I have prayed and prayed and have asked, when will you finally make this all go away for me?

And God Answered: You are not here to learn anything, I hold no need to test you, judge you, teach you. You are an aspect of the complete whole. You are manifested in your existence to remember who you are, the full realization of your truth, to awaken to the God potential that is you, my gift to you, through me, to be reunited as one. Awaken through the love I have placed within you and awaken to being one with your creator, the I Am within. Awaken through truly loving yourself. Realize that you are already with me now and your outcome is assured to total and utter joy no matter which path you take. You and I are one and together now even as I communicate with you. You choose to believe we are located in different locations as if we could ever be apart, for that is not possible.

Know that I have given you a beautiful mind to hold the thoughts you would like to experience, to see, feel and touch in your reality. You ask when will I make your life one of pure joy and worry free? In truth I am asking you the same, when will you begin to see the power of your thoughts to manifest your reality? This is why you came, to create as you desired. The simple answer is your life will change to that of joy, peace and abundance when you release yourself from the bondage of negative thought and begin to hold positive thoughts.

Sit quietly and ask for your mind to be united with me and surrender your thoughts to me, do this quietly before you begin your day and see what miracles we, together as one can create. Fearful negative thoughts such as doubts, regret, shame and guilt do not serve you and are imprisoning you to a reality of unhappiness. It is a prison of darkness you have placed yourself in. The key to freedom from your prison is within your thoughts, choose the thoughts that will make you feel peaceful, joyful and empower you to take action and unlock the door to the self made prison and walk out into the light of freedom. You are the only individual that has the ability to imprison yourself in darkness through fear and at the same time the only individual that can free yourself into the light of happiness and prosperity through love. All this is being played out before you at the level of mind where you are holding your thoughts.

You go about creating your life conscious or unconscious, either way you are always creating. There are billions of realities occurring simultaneously at this moment. Each reality is connected and creating the entire human experience, I am the reality that contains all possible realities, I am as you are, the whole of all that is. You are an aspect of the whole which is now focused into one singular reality which is you, through the body. Your spiritual being or God self resides within, for I am observing through your existence, your thoughts, emotions and actions, throughout you entire life. There are infinite amounts of realities being experienced throughout the cosmos, by endless life forms of consciousness and you are connected to all of them throughout the entire universe. All levels of creation of all dimensions of space and time are of the One, which is you and I. There is nothing to learn, no going somewhere, there is only awakening to your truth, to the full memory of who you truly are.

Me: So if I think, "God is love, I am love, God and I are one," how does this begin to do anything for me?

And God Answered: Thoughts like this will awaken you to the realization that you are limitless to create powerfully as one with me. This is a simple process I have given you to create and this should be used wisely for it can create heaven on earth.

1. Thought (God beginning) is the first level of creation.
2. Word (Gods vibrational sound) is second level of creation.
3. Deed (Gods thoughts and words moving, action) third level of creation.
   Manifestation is the result (God experienced) Reality.

This is a very simple process to create as you desire yet you allow fear and doubt to cloud this creative process. Clarity of thought is utmost necessary for this to occur rapidly. Negativity and indecision delay or do not allow your dreams to manifest and you stay stagnant in an endless cycle of repetition day in day out. This occurs because you choose not to hold steady in your faith and simply choose not to align your mind with me and hold thoughts that through God everything is possible.

Me: I have so many thoughts every day, every second I am thinking. How do I know which are the right thoughts to hold, what to think? How do I know which thoughts to hold and go with or let go?

And God Answered: I am at the very center of your being, your beautiful temple, your body, I am the observer within. To be centered with me is to feel loving, peaceful, powerful, strong, joyous, creative and prosperous. This means you are simply positive and happy, being centered with me is to know you are a being of infinite creative possibilities, a powerful creative force that knows no bounds and is limitless to create at will.

Now when you hold a thought and you do not feel positive in anyway and there is a negative charge within your wonderful temple in any way, the body will signal you through your emotions that I, the real you within, would not choose that negative thought or emotion. I know that this does not serve you and I am signaling to you that you have allowed fear to enter into your being and you are now strengthening the illusion of doubt and impossibility you have created.

When you move away from being centered with me you will feel an uncomfortable emotion which will also be felt within the body, a headache, tense shoulders, tightening in your chest, pain in your throat, a heaviness throughout the body, there are many symptoms that will be felt throughout your body. If you consciously or unconsciously continue along with thoughts of fear the body will fall prey to disease. A disease is a signal of being fully removed from your center, for all is created and experienced through the spiritual, mental, emotional and finally the physical. If you are centered with me, your body will reflect it by feeling light, easy, peaceful and happy, these are your natural states.

Me: So I created this dream, this illusion and I became so focused on it that I came to believe that I was part of it and then felt separated and abandoned. Then I allowed fear to set in which only kept perpetuating more fear and more and more of this false reality, this illusion I so believe is real. Thinking and feeling thoughts of love will cultivate self love and as my love for self grows, my illusion begins to disappear and I awaken from this dream I have created. Remembering that I and every other being are one through the same source reminds me that to fear, attack, judge or hate is to do this upon myself. If I love, forgive, cherish and hold the highest thought for all my fellow beings is to really and truthfully give it to myself. As difficult as this may seem at times I can choose love at this very moment, no matter what the circumstances of my dream appears to be. I can choose to hold loving thoughts toward myself and this will begin to lift me up spiritually, mentally, emotionally and physically.

And God Answered: My gift to you was always free will, free to think the thoughts you desire to create that which you choose to experience. Dream your dreams, for your dream will come alive by the virtue of the thoughts which reside within you and your emotions energize those thoughts and push them outward to form. This was your desire and I love you so much I deny you nothing. For I know that you are here with me now already, even as we speak. I know you, I see you, I hold you in my love at all times, which is now, there is only now and no other moment. I reside in your present moment, we are one now, you just need to awaken to this, the greatest dream you can create is to awaken from the dream of your dreams, I lovingly wait for you to awaken.

Me: I understand that self love is a way to center, align and deepen my connection to you. When I do this I am aligned with unlimited potential, unlimited creativity, unlimited abundance, unlimited knowledge and connected to the All that is. So being centered with my source I can bring forth any solution to any problem I have, resolve any issue in an quick and peaceful, loving way?

And God Answered: Yes. All begins in the mind and the mind you are not, you are beyond the mind. Together we are silent, powerful and creative, for you dictate to the mind that which you desire to observe. Your mind is like an empty computer that downloads the programs you wish to have it run for you. Program the mind consciously to observe love, peace, happiness and prosperity in your life and it shall be. The best way to do this is to sit and still the mind and be centered with me. Once you silence your racing mind begin to consciously think the programs into being. This is to use the power of your imagination.

Me: So my body is a vehicle for the spiritual me or God soul and my mind a vehicle for thoughts to come through and my emotions are a guidance system that warns me if I am centered with you. My physical body is the system through which my five known senses allow me to experience the physical world and dis-ease within me is alerting me that I am not centered. If I neglect to tend and realigned with you, this can lead to unhappiness and frustration or worse a physical break down of my body?

And God Answered: Yes.

Me: Being centered means that my spiritual, mental, emotional and physical aspects are all in agreement and aligned with you, my creator, God within, the observer experiencing and simply witnessing with no judgment on whatsoever I do?

And God Answered: Yes.

Me: Why do I experience pain if you are within me? Why don't you protect me and just tell me what to do?

And God Answered: My beautiful child to tell you what to do would be to judge you as right and wrong. In truth these are opposing realities that we created in this universe to experience up, down, left ,right, hot, cold, all polarities and the most important was love or fear. For without positive in this universe negative could not exist and vice versa and we created it just like this in order for you to know it all.

You and I conspired to create this and you should know that you are with me now. I wait for you to awaken from form, what would I possibly judge you on if none of this is real? I wait for you to awaken to this conclusion because you will see the futility in fear, hate, anger, resentment, jealousy, control, separation or any form of negative thoughts, words and actions, they do not serve you. Heaven my child is just a thought away and will be created when my children choose to think, feel and know it into being in this world.

Me: An example that my mind can comprehend, is as if my baby daughter was sleeping next to me and she is safe in my arms and she is having a dream. My daughters dream turns into a nightmare and she physically begins to cry, sweat and be tense from the fear the nightmare has caused. My daughter believes her dream is so real that she has become caught up in her dream and has become so focused on how real it all seems. Yet my daughter is safe in my arms and I am gently trying to wake her up from her nightmare so she can awaken to the truth that it was just a dream. So I patiently wait for her to awaken to know that she is here and was always perfectly safe and secure, being held in pure love by me the whole time.

And God Answered: That is a good way to think of it as.

Me: So I am in a cosmic dream and I am choosing what to experience in my dream. To experience the most perfect dream, I should consciously choose thoughts of love filled with joy, peace and abundance. Love is the highest thought I can choose for myself and all others, seeing that we are all in this dream together. Ultimately we are all connected by you within and you are in all forms of creation, then in truth there is only one dreamer?

And God Answered: Yes.

Me: I should choose thoughts of love as often as I can and consistently reach for the best thoughts of who I am and think that of all others as well?

And God Answered: Always. When you understand to see through the eyes of love nothing can hurt you, you will become the living manifestation of love. Love is eternal and unwavering and remembering to see through the eyes of love undoes the illusion of separation. Pain and darkness are illusions that fade into the light of love and cannot exist for you to experience. When you choose to see through the eyes of love you lift the veil that is blinding you and you set yourself free.

Me: Let me see if I remember this correctly. Only love is real in this reality that we are perceiving, everything else that we perceive are illusions that we have projected, they seem to be real but truly are not, like a hologram, it seems real but completely transparent. The only real presence is the love we project from within into this holographic reality. Love is the essence we were manifested from and that love is the true and only existing source that is real.

And God Answered: You have remembered well. I have stated, you are here to remember your truth, your essence, your origin. If you are still with me and understanding this, you my beautiful child are on your way.

Me: So I asked to experience an aspect of the whole, which is God and in doing so I was able to experience creation and know myself through you. I am like a spark, a particle of light, a ray of God. The best example I can think of now is our souls are like a ray of sun shine. I am a ray that reaches the earth and where that ray touches becomes what I am experiencing because that is what I am focused on. I became so focused on my little ray that I forgot to see inward and see I am still connected to the entirety of the sun. Through being so focused on my little ray I felt separated but in true reality I could not because the light that causes my ray to shine is you, so there is no separation.

If I sought out in solitude and quietness I can trace the origin of my ray, I will find that it is still connected and part of the whole sun. Further more if I took my little ray and followed it back all the way to its source I will awaken to realize I am the whole sun and that every other ray that touches earth are the billions of us that collectively make up humanity. If we each traced our ray back to its source, we as a whole are the whole sun. All of us are from the one sun and make up the entirety of the sun, we are all one. Our souls are rays of light that stem from our one and only source, you…..God.

And God Answered: Yes, there is only one source that makes all that you perceive exist, you are that source just as every other being is as well. To connect with that source all you have to do is be still and silently feel it residing within you. The source within you is Me and I am the creator of all there is. Since I reside within you than you have at your disposal the answers to all the questions you are asking silently in your mind throughout your day. If you stopped just momentarily throughout your day and reach within, your days will be so much smoother and together we can create each day to serve you and humanity as a whole as well.

You see I want nothing more than to see your life filled with love, peace and prosperity. Everything you feel and experience I am there with you at every moment feeling and experiencing the same, we are one and inseparable. You are as you state the entirety of the sun although for now you are a ray of that sun that is seeking its light within to shine it upon your life and your world. Honor that powerful ray that you are and honor it in every being you encounter for in doing so you honor the entirety of all that is, which in truth is you and I as one.

Me: How often should I do this? Sit quietly and commune with you?

And God Answered: As often as possible, in doing so you nurture your spirit like water and sunshine to a flower which strengthens and nourishes it to grow with grace, this is what it will do for you.

Me: I am thinking that mornings before I begin my day would be a perfect time, often I am off and running thinking of the days agenda and am not even conscious of what I am doing, it's like being on automatic pilot, I am dragged along by my thoughts.

And God Answered: To center yourself in the morning will allow you to choose the way you desire your day to begin. I will tell you, to begin your day with me will be of great benefit as you can give your agenda over to me and it is guaranteed to be manifested for your greatest possible outcome for your success. I am with you always even if you choose not to commune with me and will still love you unconditionally. Commune with me or not, free will is my gift to you.

Me: Before I go to bed seems like another perfect opportunity to center myself, to release any negativity that may have built up, so as not to carry it with me into the next day.

And God Answered: Yes, that would be of great value to you.

Me: So to sit quietly and be conscious of my thoughts and just let them go by, I can slow my racing mind, this sounds like meditation. Is there some specific meditation, chant, mantra or posture that needs to be done to commune with you?

And God Answered: It matters not what you call it, the important goal is to quiet the mind and still your thoughts to commune with me. Your way is up to you and is unique for every being, all ways that you mention are ways to commune with me, for there are many ways. When you reach a point in your being that you feel completely present such as when you dance, sing, paint, draw, run, exercise, climb, whatever brings you to your "now", you and I are communing and you feel alive. When you still your mind begin to listen, for I am inspiring you. Ask your questions and you will always be replied. I hide nothing from you, for how can I hide if I am everywhere.

Me: So sitting quietly in a meditative state does what for me?

And God Answered: It allows you to completely be present and aware of your entirety. It allows you to see your thoughts and this gives you awareness of your being and your emotional state. Quieting the mind brings peace to you and if done daily, you reach a state where you can enter that space of peace at any moment to center you, regardless of where you are, this empowers you. You see your thoughts are your own, although they are a part of me, my essence, my energy, this is your free will to think and create as you desire. Know that behind those thoughts is energy and behind that energy is where I reside. I have stated that from the unformed is born the formed, so when you are thinking your thoughts they are being formed from the unformed. My gift to you was free will to allow you to form me as you choose through focusing of your thoughts.

When you practice being still you will eventually reach the space of the unformed. Reaching this space is the space between your thoughts, the silence and stillness where I am. It is from this space that you are united with me in full consciousness and you vibrate this throughout your being and into your world. This takes discipline and it is one that many on your world have accomplished and they are no different than you. This is the mastery of the mind, the mastery of thought, this is your greatest power to create anything.

Know the light that is you and vanish all darkness that you have created and brought upon yourself. No other can put you in darkness, this of your own doing and no other can bring you out of darkness, they may shine their light upon you to guide you out, but the choice is always ultimately yours. Be the light you came to be, know your light and shine it upon others so they will be guided out of their darkness though recognition of their own light within. Sit quietly and see your light within expanding outwardly touching all that is and bring your light of love, peace and joy to your world, this is your power within.

RAY OF LIGHT

You began as a ray of light.

So powerful, mighty and bright.

Allowance of fear caused you to lose sight.

That is when you began to experience fright.

Since that moment you have struggled to fight.

Surrender! Surrender on this holy night.

Source stands by full of glory and might.

Waiting for you to awaken oh, little light.

I Am Powerful

Me: Does meditation bring me close to you?

And God Answered: My beautiful child, you a can never be any closer to me than at this moment. You see it's a process that you have chosen to awaken to all of this. When I say you are closer to me now more than ever, I can say this with absolute surety. The dilemma lies within because you have not come to remember this truth, so you have difficulty experiencing our oneness. Sit quietly and still the thoughts in your mind, this prepares you for your awakening to your truth. You will awaken to know you are the only one that is creating your life as a partnership through me, as well that you and I are one. You will now choose to create consciously awakened. You are so beautiful and powerful and when you awaken to this truth your struggle will come to an end and your beauty will light up your life and that of others and your world.

Me: The best way I can comprehend being centered with God is like I am walking on a perfectly smooth path and there is no friction, no resistance, no obstacles just a perfect path for me to travel and enjoy. If I begin to get distracted with negative emotions and stumble off my path and begin stepping on sharp stones and bushes with thorns, the pain I am experiencing emotionally and physically is the alarm within, warning me that I am no longer centered. This is the moment I need to gather myself, quiet my mind and see that I am no longer on the smooth path. I should adjust my thoughts, emotions, actions and get back to that wonderful smooth path I was on. I can achieve this by holding thoughts of love in my mind until I physically feel better throughout my entire body, with no resistance of any kind, then I am aligned and centered again.

If I do not consciously direct my thoughts positively and change my actions, I may move farther from my center and now along with sharp stones and thorn bushes, I am encountering deep valleys, high cliffs, and bad weather. Now my emotions are really feeling negative, I become afraid, lonely, angry, frustrated, resentful and maybe I am blaming others for not giving me the right directions and I begin to worry and hold fear. So these negative emotions are my inner guidance telling me that I am really off being centered with God and have really gone off the beautiful path I was on and no matter how bad it gets or how lost I think I am, you are there within me. You are there patiently waiting for me to return and be guided.

I simply have to quiet my mind and meditate upon you, the love and peace within that strengthens me to center myself and trust the guidance within. As I begin to feel more uplifted and hold positive thoughts about any situation is an indicator that I am heading back in the best direction for the greatest success for me to find my path and be aligned with you again. If I choose to ignore my emotions which are my indicators of the direction I am heading and self creating, then I can really lose my way and be lost in a path of unhappiness, struggle, scarcity and fear. The only reason I feel this way is because the real me within knows better and is not agreeing with all this negativity. My pain serves me to awaken me to how much I need to make changes and it is as simple as beginning to hold thoughts of love for myself. My thoughts are creating the outcome of my experience, so I should truly love and accept who I am and slowly those thoughts of love will begin to erase the negative critical thoughts I held toward myself and projected on others. As I grow stronger and confident I can overcome how difficult I let my path become and gradually work my way back to that perfect path I originally began on, no friction, no resistance, no obstacles, just a perfect path for me to travel and enjoy.

And God Answered: Yes. To be centered is to be aligned with the truth within you, the real you and that aspect of you will never fail you. For it is I that resides in you and I am eternal peace. As you think a thought and that thought makes you uncomfortable in any way, it is simply that you have become off center with me. It is like a perfect stream of love, peace and happiness has been constricted and is no longer flowing smoothly to you. The uncomfortable feeling is a signal that you have allowed fear to obstruct the natural flow of what is your true state of being, a co-creator with me. Those negative feelings you feel are indicators that I within you is signaling you what you are accepting is false and is not serving you.

It is at those moments you must muster all your strength to choose a different thought. To do this, simply recognize that uncomfortable emotion, if it is anger, say to yourself "This is anger, this is what anger feels like, I am not enjoying this feeling and I recognize that anger does not serve me, I am experiencing anger because I am holding angry thoughts and it is only because of my thoughts that I feel this way." Let whatever negativity pass through your being and release it, not allowing it to lodge itself within you so that it cannot be triggered and multiplied by a future experience.

That which you hold, love or fear grows within you. Making a simple statement to yourself in the midst of your anger quickly begins to diffuse its energy and the negative emotion begins to lose energy quickly. Now this act of recognition brings awareness to you and your thoughts, doing this you begin to release the negative emotion that almost took you over and in this moment you are bringing yourself to your center with me. When you are centered, no negativity can exist in the light of our love, negativity will vanish quickly.

Now as quickly as this negative emotion came, you recognized it and released it, so now you must consciously think new thoughts to ground you and keep you centered with me. Think thoughts of truth, you may say "Anger is an illusion, there is no need for anger, for my true existence is joy and that is the only truth, I am joyful, I am peaceful, I am with God at this very moment." Feel this through your being and smile to bring forth that loving positive emotion into your reality and allow your body to feel the vibration of your truth.

You asked to come to bring light into this world, to be the light to all other souls and assist them out of the darkness, everyone of you asked to come at this moment, the great awakening out of darkness, you all have the light of God within to awaken to the truth of you.

Flowers

Flowers weather through many things, flowers endure the cold bitter nights and the harsh winds that blow them, as well as the rains that pelt them, and at times they are seared by the suns heat. Flowers overcome many obstacles for growth and so can you. Flowers grow strong and graceful, they make our world beautiful and so do you.

I Am Beautiful

Me: The beautiful song This Little Light of Mine, has taken a much deeper meaning to me. So as a great awakened being once stated "I am the light of the world." We are all each individually the lights of the world?

And God Answered: You hold within your very heart the seeds that will one day free mankind and this world of all that is negative and dark, bringing Light to all those paralyzed in darkness. Waiting within your heart is the light of love to shine in all its glory if you allow it. You are the Light of the world and you bring forth this light by centering yourself and connecting to me and by allowing your light and love to pass through you and reach out into your world touching all creation. Do not allow your light to be dimmed, it is your source, let it shine always.

Me: So I desired to experience this life and to be here of my own free will?

And God Answered: Yes, this life and many others you have desired to experience, you have been in and out of form many life times and in many forms. Your desire was to create your experience and awaken to the truth that only love is real in this reality you have projected into existence. Understand that to bless, accept and project love into this reality in all its forms is your way to awaken out of form and in doing so you become unattached from it. Freedom from the veil that has blinded you being lifted from your eyes and awakening to your true existence will ever be closer as you awaken to the love that is you. In awakening to this you will begin to project your love into this reality and doing so brings your truth into it and undoes the veil of fear that blinds you. To detach from form is not to reject it but to accept what is and not go against it for this strengthens it and keeps you blind. The love that resides within you is what fosters your life force that brings your breath to being, that is your being. Love is your only true existence and your denial of this created the illusion of fear you are experiencing now, choose to lift the veil of fear.

Bring yourself to your center where I reside in pure joy and this is done through self love. Quiet the voice of your ego, still your mind and consciously live in love through your thoughts. You always have the choice to think thoughts of love, what thoughts bring joy to you now? Consciously think thoughts that lift you, the smile of your child, the last kiss you enjoyed, the last hug you received, whatever thought you can bring up now, feel it and raise your level of love within, think and think and hold those beautiful thoughts and fill yourself with love. Look around you and be thankful for the people, places and things that are around you now, take note of all the little blessings in your life.

Be thankful now that you are alive and for your breath, be thankful for being able to think the thoughts of love and you will open your eyes to the beauty that truly surrounds you. Feel that love swelling from deep within and this will always lift your spirit. Ask me every day to show you what my love can do in your life today and I promise you will begin to witness my works through you, for we are one.

Me: I do ask and pray all the time. Is there a specific way to pray or a perfect prayer to recite? It seems my prayers go unanswered, why?

And God Answered: All prayers are answered. No prayer can go unanswered, for you and your prayers are one and the same, I have stated there is only one which everything came forth. Your prayers are your thoughts and they originate from the same source as you. When you pray, we are praying as one, there is no right or wrong way to pray. Your prayers are the same as every other thought, just as creative and it is ultimately up to you to manifest those prayers. How strongly, truthfully and faithfully do you believe your prayers will come to pass as you pray them? This is your free will to determine. I have stated we are one, for I deny you nothing, it is up to you to see your prayers become a reality, it is decidedly upon your belief that they shall come to pass. You are the creator of your experience, for you are the experience by the thoughts you are repeating silently within your mind.

Me: So it would be true to say prayers are just thoughts in my mind?

And God Answered: Everything is vibrating at a certain frequency including your thoughts and they either radiate positive or negative energy. If you decide to pray and you do it genuinely from your heart than that is a very powerful vibrating energy that is being emitted by you. Remember those thoughts that are wrapped and felt with love and positive expectation will be manifested. Call upon me throughout your day to fill your mind with loving, positive creative thoughts and so it will be. As you pray recall the process of creating that I have stated to you, the mind is the creator through your thoughts. Remember that I am guiding you within as you pray through the emotions you experience as you do so. Know and hold absolutely no doubt that I am within you and together we can fulfill all your prayers.

Me: I understand that I choose the power of prayer. So all prayers are just thoughts, like all other thoughts and how I consciously choose to empower those thoughts energetically such as prayerful thoughts is important to manifest them in my life?

And God Answered: Yes, You are the power behind your prayers, you always have been. Your life is a canvas for you to imagine it as you desire, know that it is but fear and doubt that your prayers do not come to pass. Fear and doubt do not serve you in the creative process. Know through me all things are possible and your prayers are always answered. Your thoughts are the movers of space and time, thoughts are the paint colors and your mind the brush to create a beautiful portrait that can be your life. If you allow fear to enter your thoughts, those beautiful colors become mixed and twisted to paint a nightmare for you. Awaken and consciously allow love to always enter your mind and the portrait of your life will be one that is beyond your imagination, filled with love, peace and joy.

Rainbows

When you see a rainbow it is a reflection of your creation, the beautiful colors that make a rainbow are the colors that reside in your soul. They are a gift to you from the universe, a mixture of brilliant colors to paint a beautiful portrait which is your life.

I Am Creator

Me: So I am projecting my reality onto a world which is mirroring all of it back to me? If this is true what about all the others that are here and thinking their thoughts, wouldn't it mirror their thoughts also? Why is it that as humans we fight, kill and have wars? I am not projecting this, I do not desire this, so how am I responsible for any of this?

And God Answered: You all have been given the same ability to create as you desire. Your world is reflecting to you the whole of all the thoughts of all beings collectively back to all of humanity. Your world is in the condition it is in simply because it is mirroring what humanity is thinking collectively, as well as where you as a species are consciously at as a whole Yet you as an individual have the ultimate choice as to what your life will be, no outer circumstance can affect you as much as you may believe it does, it does not. Do not let the outer influence the inner, because the truth is my child that the inner is always reflecting to you the outer. If there is something in your reality that you do not agree with do not focus on it for that is to give more energy and life to it, rather bless it and let it go and give your thoughts and attention to that which you do desire to see in your world.

You are the creator of your world and you always have a choice and the freedom to consciously think your thoughts. Always remember that you have a choice and then choose, for indecision is a destroyer of dreams, choose and believe and it will be. Know that you are all one and to hold negativity toward any being is the same as holding it for the self and if you hold love toward any being you are truly giving love to yourself, you came here to awaken to this truth. I tell you clearly there is truly only one of us here and it may seem that there is a separation as you look upon another and that separation is an illusion you came to undo. Reside in a place of love as long as you can, do this daily for a few minutes throughout your day than gradually hourly and in time you will gain control of the thoughts you are holding and you will hold love always. The more positive thoughts and loving thoughts you hold, the more you become that love and you will be the living manifestation of love that you came to be.

Me: I should hold thoughts of love toward the self, for what I have, I can give. Let's see if I understood this, as an example I will play out a scenario to show this. I am walking home and you and I come into contact and I am holding a bag of groceries with bananas, apples and carrots and our conversation goes as follows.

God: "Hi, may I have an apple?"
Me: "Yes, have an apple."
God: "May I have a carrot?"
Me: "Yes, I have a carrot that I can give you."
God: "How about a banana?"
Me: "Sure, I have that as well to give."
God: "Thanks, by chance do you have celery that I may have?"

Me: I look within my bag and say "No, I am sorry for I do not have celery to give you." As simple as this sounds, I am that which I hold within, I can only give that which I am holding.

And God Answered: Yes, for you are the bag that is holding that which you may give and your emotions are the energy you are holding within. Thinking and holding any negative emotions as anger, jealousy, frustration and such is what you will go around giving others because this is what you are holding in your personal bag. What you hold is emanating from you and is creating your life and you do this unconsciously, you sleep walk through life and this is what is making your life difficult. Now if you choose to cultivate self love through thoughts of self love, this creates happiness, forgiveness, peace, kindness, respect and positivity within you and these are the aspects your personal bag will be filled with and as you go about your day this is what you have to give to every being and situation that you may encounter. All that you give will be given to you and will be reflected back to you.

The secret is that these are the tools that will bring the quickest most peaceful successful outcome for you. You can only give that which you hold and that which you hold is creating your experiences. Awaken now to this truth, you are the creator and giver of your reality. When you cultivate self love you become conscious of that which you are holding within and realize that what you hold is creating your experience. You will come to know that to respond negatively will only create more pain, so you awaken to the truth and decide, "I will not hold negativity within." All those painful emotions associated with negativity as fear, hate, anger, jealousy, resentment and such do not serve you and you will no longer desire to respond to life situations with these emotions, for in doing so you hurt yourself.

Me: So the inner creates the outer?

And God Answered: Always, to blame anything outside of yourself for your current circumstance in life is to give your gift of inner creation away, this is to deny the very power that is you. Remember the creation process and from within you bring into your experience the dreams you wish to see in the outer. One must give love to the self first, an honest love of acceptance and forgiveness for the self, a healthy respect of love and admiration toward the self before a shift from within can occur and this will begin to be reflected in your life.

You project your reality which you experience, every person, place, thing and occurrences. All of your life will begin to reflect the love you hold for the self, a field of energy will surround you that will touch every aspect of your life and turn everything around for your benefit, for your success, for the greatest outcome of your life and all humanity as well. As you awaken, you lift humanity as a whole. That is how important you are, you alone can raise the consciousness of your world. As you awaken you become that which you came to be, the light of the world.

Light Bearer

You came from the light, your origination was not here, the seed of life was planted on this world but you originate from beyond the stars. You came to bring light into this part of the universe, you are a light bearer to show the way home to all light bearers. You need first to walk through your own darkness for the light does not know it is light until it knows its darkness. You must fully embrace your own darkness and the darkness of all others and only then will the darkness hold no power over you, when this occurs you become the light. As stars light our dark skies, so shall you be the light onto the darkness.

I Am Light

Me: I was meditating and this thought, idea, ran through my mind. God is the unformed and loves us so unconditionally to allow us to form it as we desire, from the unformed our thoughts come from. As we have more and more thoughts after the initial thought of whatever it is we desire to manifest and we hold a continual process of those thoughts through our imagination, forms our reality.

And God Answered: Always, everything you perceive was projected from within and began as a thought.

Me: Ok, although I am still not sure how if I am creating all of this, how is the person next to me also creating all of this, I go back to the idea that I did not ask to create all the unhappiness that is occurring around the globe, how do I have anything to do with that or with the creation of others?

And God Answered: Remember there is only one and you are experiencing consciousness through a single spectrum which we chose for you to do and this agreement is the same for all other beings. Currently you see the self as you and when you look upon another as separate you accept the illusion of separation, yet the essence of all beings within is me, the same as you. Even the space which you believe separates you is an illusion, for I am the space between you as well which binds you together, I hold all beings in my space. The universe as you see it resides within my beingness, for I am everywhere, I am all that is. Awaken to the oneness from which all form came into being, if you can see the oneness and connection to all beings then you will see that you are collectively creating as one.

Your world is a reflection of all the thoughts which all beings here are thinking and holding, yet you are doing this as a whole from my perspective. Still the most important thought is of self, always hold yourself in a loving space. I need not you to believe in me, although always believe in yourself and the tremendous creative power you have within to create love in all areas of your life. This love will be reflected throughout your entire world and in all beings, to believe in yourself is to believe in me. There is no greater joy for me to know you hold pure love for yourself, as you do this I experience that love as well. This brings great joy to us both.

Me: Let me see if I can explain this in a way my mind can understand. It's like a jig saw puzzle where there is the whole puzzle, (You God) and all its pieces (Us), and I am a piece of that whole puzzle that I am focused upon. If I can see myself at a higher perspective and see the whole puzzle complete, I can see that the puzzle piece that is me completes the whole puzzle and all the other pieces are the other beings thinking their thoughts and creating the puzzle as well. When each of us sees ourselves as the whole puzzle perfectly fit together and not separated, we will see the big picture and see you as one through all of us.

And God Answered: That would be correct.

Me: Although how does seeing all as one stop unhappiness from being created in our world?

29

And God Answered: Unhappiness vanishes from the realization that you are the whole puzzle and you come together as one. All beings were created from me and are one and the same, yet there resides my personal love for you that created your distinct aspect, for no two beings are alike, just like a puzzle piece has its unique shape and form yet fits perfectly to the other pieces to create the whole. This realization will free you from the ego (false separation); you will know to hold any negativity toward any being is useless and does not serve you. When you fully come to this truth and its full realization dawns upon you, fear will leave your heart and there will only be love for the self and all others. The illusion of separation will fade away and there will be rejoicing in the heavens for you have awakened to the only reality that is and that is I, which is pure love. You will have come home.

Me: I understand now why the Golden rule of "Do unto others as you would have done on to you." appears throughout all major religions and throughout all cultures, this has taken a deeper meaning for me. A master stated "Truly, I say unto you, as you did it to one of the least of these my brothers, you did it unto me." He saw God in all beings. He saw himself in all beings and he saw the oneness of it all.

And God Answered: Yes and you will awaken to this, as all beings eventually do.

Me: Did this master achieve this because he was closer to you as the Christ, your son?

And God Answered: There you see, again you go believing in the separation. This master you refer to is no different then you and resides in you now because this being awoke from the illusion and returned to all that is. This being achieved the consciousness of being fully awakened and now resides in all beings through what you term Christ. What you refer to as Christ is simply a consciousness that is attained and allows you to see through the veil of separation that truly is not there. It truly matters not what you call it, it is simply awakening and knowing that absolutely only love is real and that love encompasses all that is. You release all fear and come to the realization that it is an illusion you chose to give life to and is not real and can no longer ever return to your holy space of pure love. This achievement is total freedom and you chose to come here to exemplify that freedom by showing your oneness to others by always holding and giving love at all times. To become the living consciousness of Christ as you term is to live in a perpetual state of love and oneness with me and see all beings as one with you.

I remind you beautiful child that is reading these words now, you chose for this information to come to you at this time to further awaken you. Be kind to yourself in thought and know you are worthy of it all, there is no lack in this universe, for lack is a disease in your thoughts. Know you are worthy of all my love and I desire for you to live prosperously, joyously and peacefully. There is no need to take from another for there is plenty of everything for every being and you must honor that and release the thoughts of fear that there is lack in your world. My child, awaken and see the oneness of at all and in doing this you will find the peace you seek. You will find that to struggle is an illusion, you were meant to create and enjoy your creations, the body was a creation to experience the love that can be created in your world. Love yourself and equally love others, as you do unto another you do unto yourself.

ONE

Every person that I see
I know is a part of me
Separated we are not
The same essence we've all got
A gift we are to one another
We are one my sister and my brother
Let go the illusion of your pain
Peace in life is what you'll gain
Learn now to quiet the mind
In that silence you will find
That your heart and soul will hear
The truth thundering loud and clear
You are love, love is the absence of fear

I Am Love

Me: Wait, let's back up a little, earlier you stated you have no need for me to believe in you, can you explain this to me please?

And God Answered: This is true, it matters not weather you believe in me or not, you are still creating, we are one and the same, believe in yourself I stated. To believe in yourself is to love yourself and I am within you, as you experience, I experience. My greatest desire for you is to love and believe in yourself, for this I experience as well and this brings tremendous joy for us. I have no need for you to worship me or punish you if you do not, this is an image you hold of me from the view point of the ego, the illusory separated self. I am all that is, there is nothing I need from you. You hold a belief that if you are good I will reward you and if you are bad I will punish you. If you would simply open your eyes and see that all of your experiences are being done unto you, by you and nothing outside of you is doing anything to you, you will master your life.

I will repeatedly tell you until it so imbedded in your mind that you are the creator of your experience. Your life is being created by you and for the most part you are doing it unconsciously, simply because you are out of the present moment. You are either mournfully regretting past events or anxiously worrying about your future. Be present, the present moment is the only existence, the present is where you will find me. Being in the present moment and being consciously aware allows you to choose the thoughts you desire and those thoughts will elicit the emotional feelings you desire and bring about experiences you desire.

No one can make you feel any emotion, good or bad. It is your thoughts that give rise to your emotions about anything. I am the observer within and as you feel, I am within you letting you know that as you feel worse, you have moved farther from your center where I reside. As you feel better, the closer you are to your center with me. Eventually you will come to realize we are one, so your belief in me does not matter but your belief in you does. Your greatest desire is total love and peace and that is no difference than awakening to my presence, it's all the same, you are all of it. There is no need to love, believe or worship anything outside of the self, it is all within. So to love and believe in your self is to love and believe in me.

Me: So the only real moment is now?

And God Answered: What other time would it be? Look at nature do you see trees and flowers wearing watches? Do you see animals running around frantically asking each other what time it is?

Me: No.

And God Answered: The only moment you truly have is now. At this moment whatever thought you are thinking, is what you are, what you will become, what will be if you choose it to be. There is tremendous power in stillness, I remind you it is from stillness that all comes forth and you simply choose what you call forth from stillness. Do you see the power in this moment, in stillness? When you bring yourself into this moment and still your mind to a level of peace, you can began to consciously choose what to think, how to feel and use your greatest gift, how to create.

Me: Yes, I do see the power in this moment, as I think it, I feel it and so I become it and this is not done in the past or in the future but in my current moment, my now.

And God Answered: Yes, for every moment that you ever had stemmed from your now. Your past is just a moment of now that has passed and no longer is and your future is only a potential that is being born in your moment of now. Neither past or present truly exist, both are illusions that take away from you present moment. Reside only in this moment, this is your greatest point for creation from where you can propel your life into magnificence.

Me: This moment "Now", is where I find you?

And God Answered: Now is your most powerful moment for change. The highest most powerful feeling you can emit through thought is LOVE, wrap every thought you hold today with love toward everyone and everything, this is the fastest way to create the reality you desire. Use the bridging process. No matter what state of being emotionally you are in, you can always move to a higher state by beginning where you are at and thinking, feeling, being, thinking, feeling, being and bridging yourself over to a positive higher state and so it will be.

Focus on the creation of your desire and not lack of having it. Where you attention goes, that's what begins to vibrate within you and so you begin to see evidence of it in your life. If you look around at your life and see all the things you do not have, you create a negative emotion within that vibrates lack and so that will be reflected in your life. If you look around and are thankful for what you do have as minimal as that maybe for some, that generates a vibration of gratitude and this will resonate out into your space and in a very short time, evidence will appear to you that there is no lack in the universe.

You move yourself simply by the power of your thoughts, through will and imagination, you move into a more pleasing environment where your needs are met. How is it that you think humanity has progressed from dwelling in caves to building and living in homes? This is evolution through thought and always will be. This is a simple process and one that must be practiced with belief, intent and discipline, for it can never fail you.

"NOW"

    Know this "now" at this moment you are being given a gift it, is your "now". Not your past or your future but your gift which truly is the present, your "now". Do not waste your "now" regretting your past it only steals the energy from your "now" and please do not worry or be anxious about your future for this too steals the energy from your "now". Choose "now" to live in neither, live only in your "now". Smile now, laugh now, sing now, dance now, hug now, tell someone you love them now, forgive now, share what you have now, raise your head in honor now, be at peace now, breathe easy now, be thankful now, feel joy now, be patient now, be understanding now, be strong now, feel alive now, cherish life now, be free now, love yourself now and most important give love "NOW"!

I Am Present

Me: So we are holding thoughts based on past events that create our current feelings and we constantly review our past in our minds and relive it. If we are not in our past we are worried about our future and by worrying we are actually creating a future with difficulties. By not being in the present moment my thoughts and feelings are dragging me through my day, like a train dragging me and me behind it. Being present allows me to be the conductor of my thoughts which is leading the train of my life where I desire it to go.

TRAIN OF THOUGHT

The Awakened Train of Thought

_ _ _ Actions---Decisions---Emotions---Thoughts---Present---I---Conscious Engine>>_ _ _ _ _ _ Freedom

The Sleeping Train of Thought

_ _ _I-Actions---Decisions--Emotions--Thoughts-Past/Future--Unconscious Engine>>_ _ _ _ _ _Imprisonment

By stilling my mind and bringing attention to my thoughts and just stopping to be aware of what I am thinking puts me in the front seat of my train of thoughts. Being aware of my thoughts allows me to have the best reaction to whatever may come my way throughout my day, instead of creating my day by default and saying and doing things I may regret, I choose how to feel, react and what actions to take for a successful day.

And God Answered: Yes, that is an excellent way to see it

Me: I know my questions sound the same, I am trying to understand this. So "Now" is the best moment to be in, this is where I am centered with you, this is where I find you?

And God Answered: I am you. I am within you, there is nowhere that I am not. The closest you can find me easiest is within you. I am your center, I am you when love is present in your being, complete joy. You allow this to occur rarely in your life and you move about not being centered and you feel the discord, the separation, the pain. These are indications that you have shifted away from me and into the illusion you have created, your false reality. Know when you are centered love is present, joy is present, peace is present.

When you are centered in your being there is no fear or any negative emotion, this is when you are your most powerful to create, to change your life, to change your world. When any negative feeling arises within you, this is the beginning of you shifting away from your center. Shifting in the slightest from your center will cause you discomfort, this is me calling you to return. When you are in pain and total despair and you feel the darkness all around you, know that you have simply shifted so off your center and into your illusion by the virtue of your thoughts. Emotional pain is your ego (separated self) pulling you away from your true self. To simply make the pain and darkness disappear bring your thoughts to the present moment and begin to hold thoughts of love, joy and peace. You must do whatever it takes to bring these thoughts in accordance to how you are feeling. Your emotions were put in place to remind you of being centered with me, when you feel emotional discomfort of any kind, quiet your mind and seek me within and I will align you with me for the best possible solution for any of your burdens.

I am your creator for we can undo all of your worries and fears so that they never manifest in your life. You must center yourself and release negative emotions and awaken to my presence within. I will repeatedly state for you to love yourself, love yourself, love yourself and forgive yourself of your past and be free of your pain, which is all of your own making. Think the thoughts you desire to think. Your thoughts are creating the emotions you are feeling and dictate the reality you experience. To be free from the pain you feel, you must love yourself. Feel the love within growing strongly and let that love bring you to this moment and you will see there is no other existence other than now and the past will be no more and you can choose to create how you feel.

Me: The pain I am holding now, how do I release it?

And God Answered: Your pain is the accumulation of your perceived misdeeds and guilt you hold as well as the misdeeds you perceived have been done unto you by others. Either way you must forgive yourself for past regrets and others for the pain you felt they caused. Forgiveness is freedom from your pain, to forgive is to live.

Me: Is there a specific task I have to do, karma I must repay, I get frustrated, what is my purpose?

And God Answered: The only need in your life is the need to come to the full realization that you are love and your only one true purpose is to love yourself fully through forgiveness. Cultivate that love within and then proceed to give that love to everyone and everything that you create. Enjoy your life as it was meant to be, creating without fear and pain. When you are deeply inspired and motivated you are centered within my presence. If you remain centered you become a powerful creative force and your inspiration must manifest, it is a law. All your greatest teachers that lifted man to a higher awareness were consistently centered and never wavered no matter what came at them. They understood I Am within, for I Am the highest God of all creation and through me all things are possible. Your greatest teachers, scientists, philosophers, inventors, those that moved your world closer to me understood this. Know when you are in fear, you are paralyzed and do not allow yourself to be centered and your misalignment brings more fear, more pain. Simply quiet your mind and bring your thoughts unto me and allow my undeniable strength and love to flow through you and all will be overcome.

To know me is to see me within you, feel me within every cell of your being, hear me within guiding you. There is not a moment I am not with you, see me everywhere and in all beings, for there is nowhere I am not. When you open your eyes and remind yourself to see me everywhere you will come to the full realization that you are my child within me, a God awakening to its full potential. You are an aspect of the highest creator, you are my reflection. All that is me, is within you. You chose to fulfill the experience of awakening within me and awakening to the truth of your God being within. You are here to remember and to awaken to the full God potential that is you and your purpose is love, to know love, to be love and to give love.

Me: What is love?

And God Answered: Love is whole, complete and lacks nothing. Love is your true being, your true essence and your home. Love is the grandest version that is you. Love is the highest manifestation that is you. My love for you is unconditional. Self love is the door to freedom from your past and the past of others. Self love is forgiveness and acceptance of the present moment and only love in the present moment is real. True love is the deep unconditional desire for every being to have joy in their life regardless of your personal condition. Love is an essence you must give to receive many folds in return. Love will free you from the veil of fear you have blinded yourself with. Love is the portal to the real you. Love is the answer to all you fear, love is what we are as one.

Me: Through being present and feeling love, I find you?

And God Answered: You find yourself, which is,.....you and I as one.

Me: Open your eyes we are all connected, we are of one race, the human race, and we are one big family. We have allowed fear to separate us. Fear is an illusion born in thought. Black, white, yellow, brown, Christian, Muslim, Jew, woman, man, straight, gay are labels that separates us if we only see ourselves as them. There is only light and that light resides in all beings and comes from one source that connects us all. When one race suffers at the hands of another race, the only true suffering that occurs is in the entirety of the human race.

And God Answered: Yes my child, you understand and to those reading these words, you asked for them to cross your path to remind you of your path. Your spark within realizes the truth of these words and they call you to awaken. To be love, to be light, to be one.

Me: My thought on love is like a muscle or skill that I must train and practice through vigilance and discipline. It is an investment that must be tended to by my thoughts, words and actions, my time and energy. We should pause throughout our day and hold thoughts of love toward ourselves then give it outwardly to our world. As I hold love for all beings, this will be reflected back to me?

And God Answered: Yes, the outer creates the inner, the outer is a mirror reflecting all that is within back to you. Would you like to have a holy encounter?

Me: Yes, I would love to have a holy encounter with you, tell me how.

And God Answered: If you desire to have a holy encounter all you have to do is look into the eyes of the nearest being and there you have it, a holy encounter. You see I reside within all beings and when you meet another, you and I are meeting and they too are meeting me (God) within you. Go now toward anyone and stand close enough that you can look into each other's eyes. Look very closely, you will literally see yourself in them. You will see your reflection in their eyes and they will see themselves in your eyes, you will see each other within each other and you will know you truly are one. You are of Me, My Love, the I AM within. I am all beings and when you see your own reflection in a glass, a mirror, anywhere, know this too is a holy encounter, honor the self and all others, all beings are children of God and all God's children deserve love.

Me: Wow, I really can see myself within another literally. You said "All beings are children of God and all God's children deserve love." So am I one with those individuals that society deems evil and dangerous?

And God Answered: Fear divides. There are no enemies, only reflections. Give love always to those that are evil individuals, these individuals deserve love the most. It is their loss of self love that created them as they have become. Lack of self love is the root cause of their self hate which in turn they project and act upon against others. Remind these individuals of their truth, of their true essence which is love, self love is the road back to redemption and wholeness for all beings. These lost souls must be given love and shown forgiveness so they can free themselves from the grips of their false ego which is perpetuating their guilt and self hate. You my child have so much love within you just as these beings do, holding your love powerfully can penetrate into the souls of these lost ones and can assist in activating their love within. In doing this you and they move toward shattering the illusion of separation and pointing each other to being whole again.

Me: I love you God.

And God Answered: Then you are remembering to love yourself.

Open Your Eyes

Open your eyes and see through your illusion

It will clear up much of your confusion

Open your eyes you are the creator of your pain

Let it all go there is so much to gain

Open your eyes, into your life bring in the light

At that moment your life will take flight

Open your eyes let you spirit soar and fly high

Live your dreams, reach your goals, touch the sky

Open your eyes, know you are much more than you believe

For you there is nothing that you cannot achieve.

If you want to know where the secret to life lies

I tell you, all you have to do is open your eyes.

I Am Complete

Me: So I should cultivate love for myself to strengthen who I am and this will be what I will hold and give. I should do this to those who hurt me and not hold judgment against them?

And God Answered: Give your love, compassion and forgiveness to those that you have felt have hurt you and caused pain in your life, this sets you free from the pain that is holding you back from a peaceful and joyous life. The love within you is an inexhaustible supply that is eternal, hold and give this love at every moment wherever it is you may be and this will clear away any surrounding negativity, this is your true power. Walk courageous and fearless with love ablaze within you and no harm can come to you.

All attacks emotional or physical in any negative form as hate, anger, jealousy, resentments, etc… are calls for help from the being perpetuating the attack, whether they are aware of it or not. Attack stems from fear, so this being is residing in fear and to be in fear is painful and if they knew their truth they would not attack. This is why all beings must be shown love, so they may see their truth in you and awaken. Their call for help is answered through your love.

To look upon and judge another's past is to hold yourself back and bring your past upon you. To forgive one's past is to forgive and free yourself from your past and guilt. You are reflections upon each other, as you see yourself you will see upon others and in return they will reflect you. There is only one of us that exist, all is one, so to hold any kind of thought toward another being is to hold those thoughts toward the self. The self is always being reflected by the thoughts one holds and this will reflect upon which beings are attracted into your space. Your family, friends, work, home, etc… And all environments are a reflection of the self, through the thoughts of one's self.

Me: I thought about everything I was being made aware of and realized something, every time I think a thought, it is I that feels the energy behind that thought. It matters not if the thought is a positive or negative thought, the energy of thoughts resonates and permeates through my entire body, shaping who I am, I become the thoughts I hold. So if I am at home angry and upset at someone that upset me earlier, that person could be out having a wonderful dinner with a friend, laughing, talking and enjoying themselves. Mean while I am at home upset, angry, insecure and replaying the same scenario over and over in my head and I am feeling sick to my stomach, I have a headache and now can't sleep because my mind is racing with negative thoughts.

Hmm… doesn't make sense that I am doing this to myself regardless if they did hurt me or not, I am the one that continues to create my own pain and they're most likely not even thinking about me at the same time. Not only am I now unhappy, I am rippling that unhappiness to individuals in my space like my family, friends, co-workers and everyday folks. By simply being unhappy, moody, insecure I affect the people around me negatively. I see how forgiveness does free me from all of this, forgiveness allows me to let go of that pain I thought a person could cause me.

43

I consciously choose not to be unconscious and let the pain over take me, I choose to release the pain and begin to feel much more pleasant and this is all simply going on in my mind…Wow. I am the one that allows myself to be hurt and feel pain or not. I am the one that is truly in control of my thoughts that leads to how I am feeling, I always have a choice to imprison myself with fear and unhappiness or be free through love and feel light, joyous and creative. I choose LOVE!!!

And God Answered: Exactly, if you can't be centered and have respect, admiration and love for yourself, how would you expect others to feel the same toward you if you can't love yourself? If you can't enjoy your own company why would others. How can you truly love another and have a healthy relationship if you do not love or have a healthy relationship with yourself. Remember you can only authentically give that which you hold toward the self. If it's not a genuine healthy love of self, then that which you give others, you might say is love, although in truth it's more of a dependence of giving and taking based on conditions, this my beautiful child is not love.

Me: It's difficult to deal with my thoughts let alone having relationships and figuring out their thoughts.

And God Answered: You are to master your thoughts only and not be concerned about others thoughts. I want you to know there is only one relationship that is of any importance and has any value and it is the relationship between you and you within (GOD). If you can really love yourself fully and stay centered and continuously stay connected, all relationships will be of equal value, you will see and know the One in all beings. If you truly love another and you tell them that you do then that encompasses understanding and patience to allow them to be who they are rather than whom you want them to be, this creates a space of acceptance for the one you love and inner peace for yourself. Remember nobody can make you feel anything. It is your reaction from within that brings about the response. When thoughts and emotions are positive you are aligned with the now eternal everlasting source (God) and pure unconditional love.

Your true happiness occurs when you discover that no other being other than you is responsible for your emotions and how you feel now. If you believe that another is responsible for the way you feel, you have made yourself a prisoner to them, because no matter how hard you try you will never be able to control how any other being may behave or feel towards you. Love, happiness, joy and peace are states of being you choose through your thoughts, you are your greatest source for love, so love yourself now and this will be reflected in all your relationships.

Me: So like anything else, to not struggle in a relationship of any kind is to fully have love for the self?

And God Answered: Yes. Discipline yourself consistently to cultivate love and happiness for the self and when your partner does the same and you come together that love and happiness is amplified. Together you create an energy field of love, peace and understanding. It will feel as you are one, no words will need to be spoken to each other, just a look into each other's eyes and all will be said. To do this you will know that your happiness is not dependent upon the other and the need to control the other is to desperately hold on to something that is not real and will always elude you. To depend upon another to fulfill you will always leave you empty, this dis-empowers you and will ultimately leave you unhappy. For two beings to come together and authentically love themselves, they will know they are literally one and as they move about the world that love will touch others. Imagine if every being, even a quarter of you did this, your reality would shift instantly, heaven will be on earth.

Me: Seeking to fall in love with another isn't that a way to find your soul mate, your other half that completes you?

And God Answered: You are already whole and need to awaken to that truth. Do not look upon another to complete you, change you, save you, for that is not love, that is imprisonment of self. You are the only individual that can complete, change, save and eventually awaken yourself. Every being serves a purpose for you, they are all holy encounters that are pushing and pulling you to awaken. Every being leads you to your truth, you asked them to be there, to assist you in your awakening. Every being you encounter is serving you to grow in self love. The beings that you struggle with most are your greatest reminders to love and awaken. Bless all beings, for through them you come to know who you are. They assist you in creating the highest version of you that you can become through accepting and loving them. What you give, you give to yourself.

Me: I understand and feel like apologizing to every being that I held a relationship with, for being angry, jealous and petty toward them or trying to control them.

And God Answered: Be gentle in thought toward yourself and be kind to yourself in action. Negative thoughts create negativity in you, positive thoughts create positivity in you and all relationships reflect you. You have now become aware and all relationships, destructive or not, needed to happen. Be thankful to those beings for you have grown from those relationships you desire to apologize for, they served you. Remember, through pain you call out for the positive, pain awakes you to make a wiser choice. A positive thought held in love is powerful and becomes unstoppable this is how powerful you are, be fearless, own your power, your gift. Begin today by choosing love, peace and compassion for yourself and all living beings. You are here to birth a new reality and it begins with you, your thoughts.

Me: Some are just rude or ignorant and I don't want to love them or put up with them, I just want them gone. What's something I can do right now in dealing with these individuals?

And God Answered: Do what you can to be present with all beings. When you are present and hold inner peace you become an immovable force of love. Being fully present allows you to see everything as it truly is and this ensure that you will remain awakened and centered with me. If you are unconscious and not centered you will meet another and see them through the eyes of the ego, you will see yourself as separate from them, which depending on your past you will judge them with anger, resentment, hate, jealousy, whichever negative emotion you hold. If centered you see them through the eyes of love, you will see the self in the present moment and this will free you from judgment.

Remember, all beings reflect you. Depending upon you and what you allow, these beings you have difficulty with will change toward you or eventually be removed from your space. You have the choice to have them reflect you as you desire and you always have. You are the creator of your relationships to all beings.

Me: So if I am centered, I am conscious of my connection to all beings?

And God Answered: Yes. See yourself in the eyes of another and know you are there with them, one life, one breath, one spirit that resides in all. Through love you awaken and lift the veil of fear and separation and see through the illusion, you will know you are all. Your fight against the self will end and the remembrance of your unity with all that is will return and great joy will rumble through the heavens as the God within awakens to the truth of its existence of always being home in pure love, light, joy and peace.

The self will no longer desire the illusion of separation because all pain stems from the original error of believing in separation. Perceive all as born again with you, to be born again is to be in the present moment and releasing the past.

Me: Not forgiving the past and all attacks upon the self or others stem from fear? .

And God Answered: Yes. To attack the past brings you out of the present. To dwell on the past keeps you in darkness and does not allow the light within you to be present, the present is your freedom from all pain. Freeing each being of their past through forgiveness frees you of your own guilt and past. As you free them, you free more of yourself from this illusion every time you forgive. Everything and everyone, no exception is reflecting the most inner you.

WHY?

Why The False Mask?

It's such a daunting task.

Why hide behind the shame?

It's such a foolish game.

Why make yourself go blind?

It's only pain you'll find.

Why is it that we don't see?

It's the truth that's sets us free.

Why do we deny our light?

It's what makes us shine so bright.

Why oh why, I ask why?

Are we so afraid to let our spirits fly?

I Am Free

Me: So this goes back to the "I am creating all of it" aspect?

And God Answered: What any being does to you, good or bad is a reflection of some aspect of you. If it is a negative act toward you, forgive them and bless them, for less of these acts will come to you. If it is a positive act towards you, give thanks and praise and bless them and more of these acts will come to you. You are creating all beings in your own experience. You are the creator of your life and your life can be beautiful and peaceful if you allow that beauty and peace to reside in you. Your world will change and reflect that beauty and peace when you bring your inner struggle to an end. To look at beings in your life and not see their past is forgiveness and to truly love them is to want happiness for those beings regardless of your own personal circumstances.

You exist in an attraction based universe. Whatever emotions you energize through your thoughts create a vibrational frequency that is sent out into your universe and magnetizes you and brings to you all that you experience. The power of your thought determines which people you attract into your life but the power of your thought also determines how you allow them to behave when they appear, you are creating it all, you all are each other's illusion. To look upon another and cast any judgment upon them is a judgment upon the self, this strengthens the illusion of separation from me and all others.

To free yourself from the illusion you have created and be released from time you must see every being with no past or guilt and free them from the illusion. You are all reflections to each other and the more beings you set free, the freer you become and the illusion fades away and the truth is revealed. Love is the connection to you and your surroundings, as love for self grows stronger it will envelop everything that is close to you, it will connect you to every being you encounter

Me: Life isn't chance, luck, coincidence, accidents?

And God Answered: Life is guided and directed by you and only you, by the virtue of the thoughts you think and hold and think upon the most. Only one person is in control of your beingness and that is you.

Me: How can I see love in my world, when there is so much pain and suffering all over?

And God Answered: Do you truly desire to see only love in this world? If this is your desire, than it is yours. Simply begin by giving love to yourself, practice this daily. Upon awakening say "good morning, I love you" to yourself and smile. When you see your reflection in a mirror, glass, anywhere, stop and mentally say to that reflection "I love you" and smile. This takes discipline but do it daily, everyday as long as it takes and feel that love for yourself. Then slowly extend that love to your immediate family, whom ever that may be, spouse, children, then friends, roommates, co-worker, strangers, pet's, nature, the planet. Simply begin with your immediate family and when you see them mentally say I love you and smile at them. Be kind and gentle with yourself in thought and how you view yourself, for your view creates who you become and those you allow into your space. Your thoughts vibrationally magnetize you to bring into your space everything you experience. You creatively people your world. The greatest gift you can give yourself is to be conscious of the quality of the thoughts you are thinking and repeating toward yourself. Know that when you forgive you release and that which you give thanks to, you create more of.

Me: Why does it seem so difficult to love?

And God Answered: Fear prevents you from giving love.

Me: Fear?

And God Answered: Yes, all negativity stems from one source and that is inner fear, which closes your heart and mind to love. Cultivating self love opens your heart and brings clarity to your mind to produce thoughts of higher awareness, which will produce thoughts for correct action and guidance for complete success in all areas of your life. Love is infallible

Me: I want to give a quick recap. My thoughts are creating everything around me and everything I am experiencing. The people, places and things are being created by my thoughts and how I feel about my thoughts energizes them to manifest a pleasant or unpleasant experience. My emotions are my guidance system telling me whether to go with that thought or not. When I think a thought and it feels negative that is a warning sign to not follow up that thought with another negative thought because it can and will manifest. It's at these moments I have to stop, still my thoughts into a different direction with positive thoughts. I get it, I really do, although at times it feels forced to say "I love this person, I love this person, I love this person" over and over in my head and still feel angry at them inside. Why?

And God Answered: Simply because there has not been an authentic shift from within, you are trying to force it with repetition and not authenticity. You can achieve this by building a bridge of authenticity from the negative to the positive. You do this by releasing the negativity incrementally, step by step or rather thought, feeling, thought, feeling, over to acceptance and positivity. This will create the inner shift from within and your outer experience will shift as well and always for your benefit.

Me: Hmm… I see what you mean, let's see if I understand this.

Let's say a mother is at home with a 1 year old baby and that baby has been crying for awhile and she is frustrated, upset and even a little angry at her child. She has become this negative form from within and the more the child cries the more irritated she is getting. It's like being caught in a cycle, the more the baby cries the more she gets frustrated, the more she's upset, the more the baby cries and on and on. At this very moment, for her benefit, she stops, just stops and watches her thoughts, then slowly begins to think her thoughts consciously.

Her thoughts can go like this. "I am experiencing anger, I am upset right now, I am frustrated, (Awareness) I am angry with my child, I know he is only 1 years old and doesn't understand that I am letting myself get upset by his cries and as I get upset with him, he cries louder, I know I am part of the cause in this, I have been through much tougher days, he's cried many times before, it always eventually ends, (Acceptance) I know that he is a sweet loving happy boy so many other times, just the other day he had me laughing so much as he played with our puppy, I love when he hugs me, I love when he tries to kiss me, I am a good mother, I love my baby, (Authentic feeling), I feel better, (Inner shift) I am going to put music on and dance with my precious boy, everything is good, I am thankful now." They dance ☺ (Outer Shift)

And God Answered: Yes, she brought awareness to her negative emotions. This brought her to a conscious state where her negative thoughts did not drag her in to more negativity that may have lead to painful consequences. As she became conscious she felt the negativity pulling her and at that moment she became aware that she has a choice to go toward the positive. She consciously chose to change her attention from negative thoughts to positive thoughts and successfully bridged herself over to the positive side to create the best outcome possible in that moment. Where you focus your attention, you energize and this expands into your reality. This is your freedom to choose, you always have a choice to bridge to the positive and experience joy.

Me: So no matter what situation I am in, I have the ability to create the best outcome?

And God Answered: Yes, awaken to this truth. I have stated not to place blame upon anything outside of you, this gives rise to more illusion that will draw you into unconsciousness. There is no experience that you cannot bridge over to a greater experience, even positive experiences can be bridged over to a higher experience and this is where inspiration is born from, in-spirit. Do not place blame upon others, establishments, corporations, religions or your governments, do not give your power away, take responsibility for your creations and change them from within to be reflected upon the outer. Do not except that someone other than you can make a difference, stop waiting to see the changes you desire to see in your world, be the example of the change you desire and it will be so. World peace begins when your inner struggle ends.

Me: I like that and I understand our outer struggle will come to an end when our inner struggle ends. World Peace begins when our inner struggle ends, our inner peace will reflect world peace.

And God Answered: Yes, these are the thoughts of an awakening being.

Me: Since our world reflects our collective thoughts, then most of our collective thoughts are of fear rather than love since many are suffering in war, poverty, starvation and disease, would this be correct?

And God Answered: Yes. The answer to all of mankind's problems is a simple one and it is self love. Most of all the beings on earth suffer not from lack of things, money or food, it appears that way although all forms of lack are a result of lacking self love. Your world is in the condition it is in due to the entirety of humanity lacking self love and it is cruelly being reflected back at you as your reality. Self love is acceptance of self, to have love, honor, respect and peace towards the self. When you attain this for the self this is what you will project outwardly toward everyone and everything and this is what will be reflected back to you as your world. When you achieve this you are aligned, centered with your creator, for I Am love, love that is barely known or felt in your world.

When you center yourself and are aligned with me, my promise to you is that all your needs will be met, you will lack nothing. When you bring your mind to a quiet place and hold thoughts of love, know you are in my presence and when this occurs I fill you with a love that you have not known and this love will flow through you and out into your world. You become the light you so desperately seek, the light within you is what projects out and creates for you, through this you will create what you desire and have all your needs met.

Me: What can I do right now at this moment to create peace on earth?

And God Answered: Simply love yourself, this will radiate outward and affect your world. You will emanate the vibration of love and this raises the collective consciousness of your world. Through love all problems have solutions if you stop running from them. The most amazing changes can come from the most terrible truths if we come together and have the courage to look at them. The darkest illusion that has fallen upon you is that mankind has limitations. United you are free, divided you are conquered. Every thought you hold is so powerful in creating your collective reality. Be conscious of your thoughts, master them and hold inner peace, for you are a crucial piece in guiding your world toward world peace now.

She Cries

She cries, for we all make her weep
She is scarred all around, her wounds are deep.
She cries, for her children have gone blind
The truth they lost, we are all of the same kind.
She cries that it is getting too late
The virus has spread all around and it is hate.
She cries that the end maybe near
All this destruction stems from our fear.
She cries as we destroy the seeds of life
She bleeds slowly as if cut by a knife.
She will cry no more when we give up our fight
And awaken to realize we are all one and unite.
She is the one who gave us birth
Give her love, she is mother earth.

I Am Peace

Me: So evil is within and part of God?

And God Answered: I tell you now for evil to exist outside of me would be to believe there is something other than the I Am, the all that is. Where would evil come from? For evil came to be from fear, evil is simply the fullest manifestation of fear and yet it is within the I Am. Evil exists only because it is energized through negativity. Individuals that you see as evil are beings that have so obstructed their connection to me from the fear they hold within. What you term an evil being has my light within. All negative, hateful and angry beings do, they are simply unconscious of their truth. These are beings that have brought darkness upon them but none the less my light and love resides within them. To these beings bring your love and light. For what occurs when light is brought to darkness?

Me: The darkness vanishes?

And God Answered: Yes, always. Do not hold fear in the face of what you term evil. When you are centered you cut right through the illusion of those that do evil deeds for behind that monstrous façade is a being so filled with fear and self hate they are calling out for help by their awful actions. These beings have fallen prey to darkness that convinced them they are unworthy of love and so their decent into self hate began. No being is evil, just unconscious of their truth. Evil is the illusion that seduced them, yet all evil can be bridged to the only existence of love. Let those you perceive as evil know they are loved, this will slowly chip away at the dark thick exterior that is obstructing them from seeing their inner light. A simple constant stream of water can erode a mountain side, this simplicity is its power, just as the power of constant love will always erode any evil. None of my children are evil just blinded of their truth.

Me: Is money the root of all evil?

And God Answered: Money is a collectively accepted created system that is empowered by your choice to do so, for that is simply what it is, a created system. It is neither good nor bad. Money is an object that was created by the mind just as a knife was. A knife can be used to kill your brother or cut your vegetables into a beautiful salad. A knife in itself can do nothing, just as your money. Money in itself can do nothing unless you give it its power to affect your world. Money can assist in feeding millions or it can be hoarded to starve millions, it is relative. All things in your world can be used to either damage humanity or move humanity to its greatest version of itself. There are many other created systems that differ vastly throughout the universe, it is all evolutionary. Evil is an illusion that is energized through negative force and will always collapse upon itself, it is created by belief in it, through your free will. The root of all evil is given rise to by an unconscious being that is filled with fear.

Me: So you do not condemn hate, anger, theft, lying, cheating or any damaging action that we do unto each other. You're saying this is neither good nor bad. I expected you to tell me right from wrong?

And God Answered: Good and bad are polar opposites created in this universe for you to experience, to choose and to make decisions upon. It is your perception to do as you will with it. I have stated before I reside in the unformed and stillness. I love you so unconditionally I allow you to bring me out of the formless and into form, it is your free will, your choice to create me as you desire. If you chose to create machines to kill millions, you can, if you choose to create machines to feed, clothes and shelter millions, you can.

It's all creation coming from you, although it is you that will experience the outcome of those creations, what you term good or bad, evolution or death. It is all ultimately up to you, I do not sit and judge anything that you do, I tell you now judgment day will never come but your awakening to me will. When you awaken to see the pain many of your creations cause and you can no longer bare that pain you will choose not to create from pain or fear. You will realize that you are doing this all to yourself and you will choose to create through love and you will experience love.

Experiencing what you call bad allows you to choose different or wiser, as you realize the bad does not serve you. When the pain becomes so great, the pain serves to wake you to make a better choice, this is how you choose to evolve as an individual or united. The bad serves you, to point you toward the good. If you consciously turned your focus to all the good in your life that is what will expand and be seen more of in your reality.

Me: This saddens me a little because I see now that we have been choosing to create from pain and fear. You never abandoned us, you allow us to create you as we desire, from the formless into form. In a sense we are mis-creating and that is why I see the negativity, the wars, the poverty, the disease, greed. It's not you God, it's us, and we are doing it to ourselves. I am so sorry and I feel ashamed.

And God Answered: Do not feel shame or guilt, this does not serve you. For you will create out of shame and guilt and continue the cycle of pain. Be aware of your choices and your responsibilities, forgive your past and let it go and simply choose again, create again out of love. States of positivity or negativity are created within and projected out and created for you to experience. When you are finally so tired of feeling the pain and that pain reaches a point that you can no longer live with yourself, know that you are near awakening. Pain serves you, it brings you to a point where you must choose to evolve or die. You all do this individually and collectively as a whole and the more each of you chooses to live in love and not fear, the closer you bring all of humanity to evolution with me. As you personally awaken you evolve all of humanity. This is how important you are, as you awaken you personally lift humanity as a whole closer to creating heaven on earth, this is why you came.

Me: What is the correct religion?

And God Answered: The religion of you, which is love. Know yourself, love yourself and be centered within yourself. Tell that fearful doubting voice within to go away and hold your mind in silence and in that quietness you will know me as you. Your truth will never be found outside of yourself from anyone or anything, your path to freedom is within. Your individual path is yours and yours alone and ultimately leads you to the path of transcendence from form back to me. To be still in mind and body will move you into quietness where all questions you seek are answered. Nothing outside of you can make you free or give you everlasting joy. Turn inward in quietness toward me and you will be given guidance to free you from yourself imprisonment. In truth, the door to your prison is wide open and you have allowed fear to enter your thoughts that have paralyzed you from freedom. Everything is leading you back to me. Every person, place, thing, experience, circumstance, situation, everything is leading you back to me whether you realize this or not.

In truth, I am not even a God to you, for you are your own God within. I, we, are one in the same, there is only oneness. For I to be your God would be to separate us and you reside within me. There is only One and all is connected or extensions of the same One, that is I, that is you, that is us in totality. I am because of you and you are because of me. My most beautiful child awaken to all we have discussed and the journey becomes a blessing.

Me: With all my heart I am grateful for all I have awakened to, thank you.

And God Answered: Your thoughts are so powerful for they reconstruct the entire universe around you as you see it. Your mind is a vehicle for the projection of thought which vibrationally moves matter into being. Your life is simply a projection of the thoughts and beliefs you are holding. All thoughts have a positive or negative vibrational frequency that is being projected from you. Be aware of the thoughts your mind is projecting and the feelings those thoughts evoke, this is a simple way to change your life. Choose to think the thoughts you desire to see in your life and it will be so, this must be done through utter belief and faith within you. The power is always you. There are deeper truths to awaken to, for you are eternal and together we will discover those truths. For the one thing I truly desire for you is to always feel loved. Know I am with you always.

Me: Dear reader, I am honored that we walked together for a moment to share this with you. Your path is your own, although I may walk with you for a while, I do go off on my own path, inevitably though we meet again at the end of our paths, they all lead to the same destination……. Awakening to God.

<u>I AM</u>

I am a spiritual being having a human experience. I am consciousness experiencing a point of my I am. I am experiencing a part of the whole, in truth I am the whole. I am the I am.

I AM

_____

(State that which you desire to be)

THOUGHT, WORD, DEED

For you if pain is what life has brought.

Sit quietly now and choose a new thought.

It is a universal law which is a simple fact.

Thoughts are what cause our emotions to act.

The simple statement of thought, word, deed.

This tool that creates life, is all you need.

Be conscious of your thoughts as a creative force.

All stems from God within, your only source.

Know you are the master of life if you master thought.

This is the secret to life which you have always sought.

THOUGHTS

You are creating your life by the thoughts you hold, which lead to the emotions you have, which lead to the decisions you make, which lead to the actions you will take, which lead to the reality you experience.

Be conscious of your thoughts

YOU

YOU are in the position YOU are in life because YOU and only YOU put yourself there, not because of anyone or any circumstance. YOU did it, accept it! YOU and only YOU have the power to change that regardless of what anybody else says or does.

Accept this and bridge to an extraordinary life

REACTION

Your reaction is the most powerful choice you make when any event enters your life, if you react with fear it is inevitable that the outcome will be fearful, if you react with love, acceptance, determination, discipline, focus and will, it is inevitable that the universe will deliver an outcome that far exceeds your expectations.

Think wisely before you react

FORGIVENESS

Forgiveness is not for those that hurt you. Forgiveness is for the self to be freed from your past and the past of others. Pain, hate, anger and depression can only visit you as long as you allow them to reside in your thoughts. Forgiveness allows you to free yourself from those negative emotions and turns them into Love, Peace and Happiness for yourself.

Forgiveness is Freedom

Loved

Love, Peace, Happiness and to shine bright.

My loved one this is your birthright.

You are strong, powerful and in control.

Give the world your love, you reap what you sow.

There are many who are lost and filled with fright.

Go out to our world and be their guiding light.

And when the darkness comes to strong.

Think thoughts of love, the darkness can't last long.

You make up your mind, when, where, and how.

Give the world your best, live in your now.

Live your dreams, reach your goals, touch the sky.

Seek within, you are loved, never say goodbye.

I Am One With God

SELF

POSITIVE

NEGATIVE

Love-Joy-Peace-Forgiveness
Acceptance-Determination
Discipline-Focus-Will

YOU CHOOSE

Fear-Hate-Anger-Blame
Resentment-Depression
Worry-Guilt-Shame

SELF FREEDOM

SELF IMPRISONMENT

THOUGHTS

Spiritual Freedom

Spiritual Imprisonment

Mental Freedom
Emotional Freedom
Physical Freedom

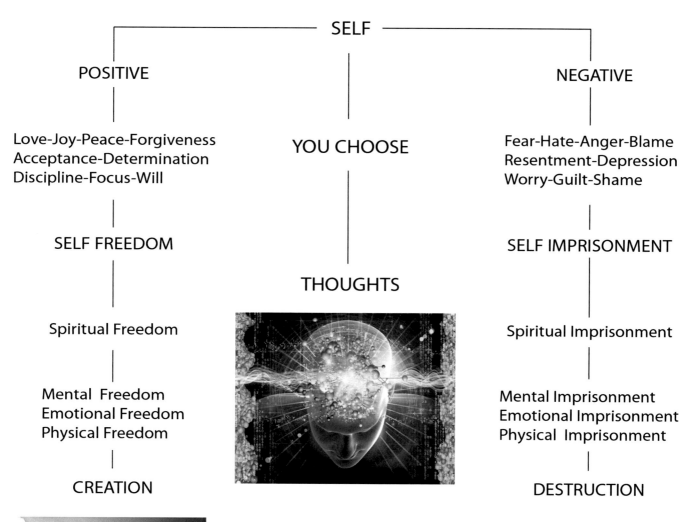

Mental Imprisonment
Emotional Imprisonment
Physical Imprisonment

CREATION

DESTRUCTION

You are the Creator of
your life by your thoughts

PEACE

World peace begins when your inner struggle ends

Inner Peace reflects outer Peace

Know that when you are upset with someone and you decide to give them a "Piece" of your mind in truth what you are doing is giving away the "Peace" of your mind.

Printed in the United States
By Bookmasters